THE COMMONWEALTH NATIONS

BIRTH FROM CRUMBLING BRITISH EMPIRE AND COLONIZATION

David I. Wood

THE COMMONWEALTH NATIONS

BIRTH FROM CRUMBLING BRITISH EMPIRE AND COLONIZATION

BY

DAVID I. WOOD

Preface

One of the earliest political unions of states is the Commonwealth. Its origins may be traced back to the British Empire, a time when Britain governed several nations. Different British Empire nations attained varying degrees of independence from Britain throughout time. Dominions were the term for nations that were only loosely allied. Beginning in 1887, dominions' leaders joined Britain for talks.

The Commonwealth is distinct from other international organizations like the World Trade Organization and the United Nations. It lacks written rules and a constitution. The group's members are bound together by common customs, institutions, and experiences as well as economic self-interest; they do not have a formal or legal commitment to one another. Actions taken by the Commonwealth are dependent on member input, which takes place via meetings and letters. Each member nation sends a high commissioner, a kind of ambassador, to the capitals of the other members.

In this beautiful illustrated book, David I Wood delves into the origin of COMMONWEALTH and its nations and the roles of the British monarch in the commonwealth

Contents:

Chapter one

How the Commonwealth was formed

The family of countries that emerged from the British Empire is best appreciated when the word "Commonwealth" is used in current contexts. Before the American Revolution, it was originally used to refer to Britain's colonies, and British leaders sometimes used it to refer to colonies within the empire in the nineteenth century. The term "colony" was deemed insulting to the position of Australia, Canada, New Zealand, and the collection of nations that would soon become the Union of South Africa by the early 20th century. All four of them had internal self-government under control and were on the verge of achieving informal if not legal independence. These countries and Britain engaged in negotiations in 1907 under the leadership of Canadian Prime Minister Wilfred Laurier (1841–1919), who came to the decision that they would henceforth be referred to as the Dominions.

The Commonwealth's central region was thereafter the Dominions. The idea's creators, including South African leader Jan Smuts (1870-1950) and British novelist Lionel Curtis (1872-1955), felt their restructuring of the empire would provide a remedy for the risky situation that Britain faced in the early 20th century. At this point, Britain had reached the pinnacle of its relative dominance and was up against strong competitors in Europe, particularly Germany. The Dominions had to contribute to the expense of equipping the Royal Navy if Britain was to stay up with these nations. However, since the Dominions were independent and often located distant from the majority of Britain's competitors, they could not be coerced or readily intimidated into contributing. In addition, if they so wanted, they would naturally demand a say in how British policy is decided.

Curtis thought that imperial federation was the answer. In the end, he was right when he said that the empire had to decide whether to remain together or fall apart. Few had such lofty goals. However, Curtis' reasoning was generally accepted and had served as the foundation for prior ideas, such as Joseph Chamberlain's (1836–1914) attempts to foster imperial unity via tariff reform after 1903. Where Curtis and others of like thought differed from Chamberlain was in their focus on the idea of self-government and how it might be reconciled with a sharing of imperial duties via the Commonwealth, which they found lofty and even utopian. Cynically speaking, the Commonwealth would slyly bring about federation; idealistically speaking, it would reshape the identities of the countries that made up the empire so that they would collaborate amicably.

The First World War simultaneously strengthened the Dominions' and the empire's connections to Britain and exposed new weaknesses in them. Britain declared war on the Allies on behalf of the Dominions and the Indian Empire, who all participated in the fighting and suffered thousands of deaths. This experience, along with the economic and political strains of the war, led to unrest in India and provided the Dominions compelling extra reasons to consider themselves the home of various, though friendly, nations rather than just Britons who were living overseas. The Dominions' representation at the Versailles Peace Conference by the British as well as their own, distinct delegations was another indication of how near to actual independence they were.

DECOLONIZATION

1960 served as a milestone year. Even in the late 1950s, the British thought their African Empire may endure into the 1970s, despite the fact that it had been obvious since 1945 that the British Empire was coming to an end. The independence granted by France to thirteen colonies and the adoption of United Nations Resolution 1514 on the abolition of colonialism in 1960 both permanently altered the environment of imperialism. Similar to the French, Britain accelerated decolonization. In 1957, Ghana joined as the first country from Africa. In the same year that Nigeria, the most populous country in Africa, gained independence and joined the Commonwealth, Prime Minister Harold Macmillan spoke in the South African parliament about the "winds of change" that were sweeping the continent.

The Commonwealth battled with the problems of decolonization over the next thirty years. Identifying the link between the British Crown and the Commonwealth became difficult as the number of prospective republics within the Commonwealth increased. At a conference of Commonwealth prime ministers in 1949, it was resolved surprisingly quickly with an understanding that the Crown would serve as "the emblem of the free association" of Commonwealth Members and, "as such, Head of the Commonwealth." As a result, a Commonwealth Member would not necessarily need to reevaluate its standing within the Commonwealth if and when it chose to become a republic.

Other issues brought on by decolonization were handled less precisely. The most challenging of them were issues with citizenship and race. The apartheid state of South Africa quit the Commonwealth in 1961, anticipating future conflicts, since it refused to accept newly independent African nations and their diplomatic representations as full-fledged Commonwealth members. The withdrawal of South Africa was a crushing blow for many Commonwealth enthusiasts, proving that the former Commonwealth was ended.

The internal policies of a specific member were not a reasonable cause for worry for the remainder of the Commonwealth, according to that Commonwealth's guiding concept. Only vehement, public debates over domestic policy appeared to be what the new Commonwealth promised. The final wave of support for the Commonwealth was also partly sparked by South Africa's exit and, more generally, by the fast transformation of the Commonwealth into a multiracial organization. The Commonwealth was meant to provide an example of peaceful coexistence amongst independent Anglophone democracies in earlier decades; in the post-decolonization age, it was expected to serve as a blueprint for coexistence among all races.

This idealism did not last through the 1960s in its prime. The Commonwealth was already losing favor with British conservatives. The effective removal of the Crown link was attacked by some, who thought it had led to the creation of a Commonwealth that stood for little more than its own existence. Others understood that keeping the Commonwealth, or even the empire, as a legitimate political entity entailed that people from Africa and Asia would have unfettered access to travel to Britain. Consecutive British administrations tried to impose control over national borders via a succession of laws, beginning with the 1962 Commonwealth Immigrants Act, without offending either Commonwealth members or supporters at home or liberal opinion.

The Commonwealth underwent tremendous transformation as a result of the quick decolonization that occurred after 1945. In 1948, Ireland proclaimed itself a republic and departed the union. As a republic with no ties to the Crown, independent India aspired to stay in the Commonwealth. Britain made changes to the Commonwealth's structure to keep India in the fold because it was determined to use the organization as a tool for informal influence. A Commonwealth of Nations was established in 1948 when the name "British" was deleted, and the London Declaration of 1949 proclaimed that the monarch was just the figurative head of a Commonwealth of freely linked nations. India remained in the organization as a result, and the precedent permitted following postcolonial governments like Ghana and Nigeria to join as well.

In the 1900s, tensions arose between Britain and its former colonies over matters of immigration, foreign policy, and sanctions against South Africa's apartheid regime. But there were other instances of collaboration that worked well. Several trusts and organizations supported by the Commonwealth have given developing countries in the organization financial support as well as economic and technical guidance. The Commonwealth has also taken political action, offering a venue for talks to end white rule in Rhodesia in the late 1970s and putting penalties on nations like Nigeria and Zimbabwe for violent and undemocratic behavior.

The British treasury was so fragile after World War II that it was unable to function without American assistance. Joseph Chamberlain's early 20th-century vision of a global empire that could unite Imperial preference, mutual defense, and social expansion was further undercut by the loss of defense and financial functions. In addition, the United Kingdom's once-vast influence on international affairs shrank more and more, particularly after the loss of Singapore and India. According to Krishnan Srinivasan, British policymakers first believed that the Commonwealth would help them maintain and expand their power, but they eventually lost interest in the idea. As British policies were criticized during Commonwealth meetings, the initial euphoria faded. As immigration from non-white member nations increased in volume, public sentiment became uneasy.

ORGANIZATION AND ACTIVITY

The Commonwealth is distinct from other international organizations like the World Trade Organization and the United Nations. It lacks written rules and a constitution. The group's members are bound together by common customs, institutions, and experiences as well as economic self-interest; they do not have a formal or legal commitment to one another. Actions taken by the Commonwealth are dependent on member input, which takes place via meetings and letters. Each member nation sends a high commissioner, a kind of ambassador, to the capitals of the other members.

The Commonwealth's principal decision-making body is its member nations' heads of state. Historically held by the British Crown, the Head of the Commonwealth title is mostly ceremonial. The Heads of Government choose who will succeed whom in the position; it is not a hereditary position. The secretary-general-led Commonwealth Secretariat manages the organization and coordination of Commonwealth initiatives as well as member state interactions. The Board of Governors, which is made up of the high commissioners of the member nations to the United Kingdom, is accountable to the Secretariat. The Commonwealth is represented at important international gatherings by the Chair-in-Office, which alternates between member nations every two years.

Every two years, the Commonwealth Heads of Government meet. Members of the Commonwealth reaffirmed its voluntary and cooperative character and vowed to advance world peace, combat racism, oppose colonial dominance, and lessen income disparities in a statement that was approved at the Singapore summit in 1971. At the summit in Harare, Zimbabwe, in 1991, leaders reiterated this stance, further pledging the group to uphold human rights and democracy. The Commonwealth was charged with creating a charter in Perth, Australia in 2011. The charter, which included fundamental values including democracy, human rights, freedom of speech, sustainable development, access to health and education, and gender equality, was accepted at the end of 2012.

Government and private British investments abroad total enormous sums throughout the Commonwealth. The trade advantages of member nations started to decline once Britain entered the European Economic Community (later replaced by the European Union [EU]) in 1973. Currently, the EU and Commonwealth nations have trade agreements. Malta and Cyprus are both EU and Commonwealth members, and they stayed in the EU when the UK withdrew in 2020. Exports from Commonwealth nations are often sent to other members. To encourage investment on that continent, the Commonwealth Africa Investment Fund was founded in 1996. The Commonwealth and its members have strong educational ties since many British professors go abroad and many students from Commonwealth nations study in the United Kingdom. The Commonwealth Games, a sports event conducted every four years, is one example of another cultural connection.

HARARE   COMMONWEALTH,   DECLARATION,   1991

(Issued by Heads of Government in Harare, Zimbabwe)

1. The Heads of Government of the countries of the Commonwealth, meeting in Harare, reaffirm their confidence in the Commonwealth as a voluntary association of sovereign independent states, each responsible for its own policies, consulting and co-operating in the interests of their peoples and in the promotion of international understanding and world peace.

2. Members of the Commonwealth include people of many different races and origins, encompass every state of economic development, and comprise a rich variety of cultures, traditions and institutions.

3. The special strength of the Commonwealth lies in the combination of the diversity of its members with their shared inheritance in language, culture and the rule of law. The Commonwealth way is to seek consensus through consultation and the sharing of experience. It is uniquely placed to serve as a model and as a catalyst for new forms of friendship and co-operation to all in the spirit of the Charter of the United Nations.

4. Its members also share a commitment to certain fundamental principles. These were set out in a Declaration of Commonwealth Principles agreed by our predecessors at their Meeting in Singapore in 1971. Those principles have stood the test of time, and we reaffirm our full and continuing commitment to them today. In particular, no less today than 20 years ago:

- we believe that international peace and order, global economic development and the rule of international law are essential to the security and prosperity of mankind;'

• We believe in the liberty of the individual under the law, in equal rights for all citizens regardless of gender, race, colour, creed or political belief, and in the individual's inalienable right to participate by means of free and democratic political processes in framing the society in which he or she lives;

• we recognize racial prejudice and intolerance as a dangerous sickness and a threat to healthy development, and racial discrimination as an unmitigated evil;

• we oppose all forms of racial oppression, and we are committed to the principles of human dignity and equality;

• we recognize the importance and urgency of economic and social development to satisfy the basic needs and aspirations of the vast majority of the peoples of the world, and seek the progressive removal of the wide disparities in living standards amongst our members.

5. In Harare, our purpose has been to apply those principles in the contemporary situation as the Commonwealth prepares to face the challenges of the 1990s and beyond.

6. Internationally, the world is no longer locked in the iron grip of the Cold War. Totalitarianism is giving way to democracy and justice in many parts of the world. Decolonization is largely complete. Significant changes are at last under way in South Africa. These changes, so desirable and heartening in themselves, present the world and the Commonwealth with new tasks and challenges.

7. In the last twenty years, several Commonwealth countries have made significant progress in economic and social development. There is increasing recognition that commitment to market principles and openness to international trade and investment can promote economic progress and improve living standards. Many Commonwealth countries are poor and face acute problems, including excessive population growth,

crushing poverty, debt burdens and environmental degradation. More than half our member states are particularly vulnerable because of their very small societies.

8. Only sound and sustainable development can offer these millions the prospect of betterment. Achieving this will require a flow of public and private resources from the developed to the developing world, and domestic and international regimes conducive to the realization of these goals. Development facilitates the task of tackling a range of problems which affect the whole global community such as environmental degradation, the problems of migration and refugees, the fight against communicable diseases, and drug production and trafficking.

9. Having reaffirmed the principles to which the Commonwealth is committed, and reviewed the problems and challenges which the world, and the Commonwealth as part of it, face, we pledge the Commonwealth and our countries to work with renewed vigor, concentrating especially in the following areas:

- the protection and promotion of the fundamental political values of the Commonwealth: democracy, democratic processes and institutions which reflect national circumstances, the rule of law and the independence of the judiciary, just and honest government; fundamental human rights, including equal rights and Opportunities for all citizens regardless of race, colour, creed or political belief;

- equality for women, so that they may exercise their full and equal rights;

- provision of universal access to education for the population of our countries;

- continuing action to bring about the end of apartheid and the establishment of a free, democratic, non-racial and prosperous South Africa;

- the promotion of sustainable development and the alleviation of poverty in the countries of the Commonwealth through:

  ❖ a stable international economic framework within which growth can be achieved

  ❖ sound economic management recognizing the central role of the market economy; effective population policies and programmers of sound management of technological change;

- the freest possible flow of multilateral trade on terms

10. To give weight and effectiveness to our commitments, we intend to focus and improve Commonwealth co-operation in these areas. This would include strengthening the capacity of the Commonwealth to respond to requests from members for assistance in entrenching the practices of democracy, accountable administration and the rule of law.

11. We call on all the intergovernmental institutions of the Commonwealth to seize the opportunities presented by these challenges. We pledge ourselves to assist them to develop programs which harness our shared historical, professional, cultural and linguistic heritage and which complement the work of other international and regional organizations.

12. We invite the Commonwealth Parliamentary Association and non-governmental Commonwealth organizations to play their full part in promoting these objectives, in a spirit of co-operation and mutual support.

13. In reaffirming the principles of the Commonwealth and in committing ourselves to pursue them in policy and action in response to the challenges of the 1990s, in areas

where we believe that the Commonwealth has a distinctive contribution to offer, we the Heads of Government express our determination to renew and enhance the value and importance of the Commonwealth as an institution which can and should strengthen and enrich the lives not only of its own members and their peoples but also of the wider community of peoples of which they are a part.

Chapter two

How the Commonwealth arose from a crumbling British Empire

One of the earliest political unions of states is the Commonwealth. Its origins may be traced back to the British Empire, a time when Britain governed several nations. Different British Empire nations attained varying degrees of independence from Britain throughout time. Dominions were the term for nations that were only loosely allied. Beginning in 1887, dominions' leaders joined Britain for talks.

The foundation of the Confederation of Canada on July 1, 1867, was noted by Queen Elizabeth II as the "first Independent nation inside the British Empire" in her 1959 speech to Canada on Dominion Day. Thus, it also heralds the founding of the Commonwealth of Nations, a free alliance of independent governments, she said. Lord Rosebery called the British Empire, which was transforming as some of its colonies gained greater independence, a "Commonwealth of Nations" in 1884 while touring Australia. The first meeting of British and colonial prime ministers took place in 1887, and further meetings led to the establishment of the Imperial Conferences in 1911.

The imperial conferences served as the foundation for the Commonwealth. Jan Smuts, who proposed the term "the British Commonwealth of Nations" and described the "future constitutional relations and readjustments in essence" at the Paris Peace Conference of 1919, which was attended by representatives from the Dominions as well as the United Kingdom, made a specific proposal in 1917. The Anglo-Irish Treaty of 1921 gave the phrase its first official imperial sanction when it changed the wording of the oath sworn by parliamentarians from the Irish Free State to British Commonwealth of Nations instead of British Empire.

In contrast to other formal international organizations, the Commonwealth has more of a family feel than it does of an alliance or contractual agreement. This sense of belonging has been emphasized by a number of Commonwealth presidents and prime ministers as well as by Queen Elizabeth II, the organization's head. The Commonwealth exists because its members believe they have a strong, innate bond, similar to that of a family. The Commonwealth relationship made it feasible to carry out its development-related activity.

Because of their shared history, same language, and increased ability to trust one another despite their differences, members regard the bond as natural. Through this connection, they have helped each other grow and collaborated to establish international agreements on important topics including trade, debt, gender equality, the environment, the danger of terrorism, and the international financial system.

In 1965, the Heads of Government founded the Commonwealth Secretariat. Although it coordinates cooperative and consultative activities and serves as the primary administrator for Commonwealth business, it lacks the authority to take the lead on high-level policy. The Secretary-General, Chief Emeka Anyaoku, is now in charge of the Secretariat and is chosen by the Heads of Government. Political matters, economic and social affairs, and development cooperation are within the purview of his three deputies. There are 13 departments, which address a variety of economic issues as well as legal and constitutional issues, women's and youth issues, science and technology, and others.

The Secretariat's budget for 1996–1997 was around £10 million, and it was funded using a scale of assessments based on population and income. 30% of the total is paid by the UK. Commonwealth election monitoring is the responsibility of the Political Affairs Division, along with arranging CHOGMs and other political gatherings. Additionally, it maintains an office at the UN in New York that smaller member nations may use if they otherwise couldn't afford to have a representative there. Other divisions organize collaborative initiatives, particularly in the field of development work, and provide training opportunities, seminars, and study tours. A Commonwealth Fund for Technical Cooperation exists in this region, with an annual budget of around £25 million, to which the UK again provides 30%.

There are numerous other Commonwealth organizations, including the Institute of Commonwealth Studies (a Russell Square center for postgraduate study on Commonwealth topics), the Commonwealth Agricultural Bureaux (International), and societies and associations in industries like health, education, law, public administration, science, the media, and youth development.

The British Empire gave way to the Commonwealth as an organic development. In the middle to late 19th century, the empire started implementing "responsible government" in parts of Canada, Australia, New Zealand, South Africa, and Ireland. Under this system, the governor could only act in domestic matters on the advice of ministers who had the support of the elected chamber. These dependent but independent nations acquired increasing levels of sovereignty, and only a British veto could limit their independence. These states were to be regarded as "autonomous communities within the British Empire, equal in status, in no way subordinate one to another in any aspect of their domestic or external affairs, though united by a common allegiance to the Crown, and freely associated as members of the British Commonwealth of Nations," according to the Imperial Conference of 1926. The decisions adopted at both that and a second meeting were formalized by the Statute of Westminster (1931), which gave each dominion the authority to manage its own internal and international affairs and to create its own diplomatic corps.

The designation "British" was eliminated in 1946, and the group was renamed simply the Commonwealth of Nations. The Statute was approved by Australia and New Zealand in 1942 and 1947, respectively. When India gained its independence in 1947, the new nation wanted to establish a republic and do away with the monarchy as the form of government. In the London Declaration of 1949, the condition that members regard the monarchy as their head of state was changed to the need that nations merely acknowledge the monarchy as the Commonwealth's head of state.

With this modification, more nations joined the Commonwealth when they attained independence from the United Kingdom, bringing the total to fifty-four today. Thirty-three of the fifty-four are republics (like India), five are independent monarchies (like Brunei Darussalam), and sixteen are constitutional monarchies with the British monarch as their head of state (such as Canada and Australia).

Although being a former dependency of the United Kingdom or a dependency of a dependency is a requirement for membership, Mozambique, a former colony of Portugal, joined the Commonwealth in 1995 under special circumstances because it was willing to support the Commonwealth's fight against apartheid in South Africa.

A RESULT OF HISTORICAL CONTEXT AND WISDOM

The Commonwealth of today did not necessarily arise through time. It was created as a result of the strong relationships that grew between leaders and people, particularly during the decolonization process and the early stages of the Commonwealth's development as a group of independent republics. There have been multiple such turning times, but Jawaharlal Nehru's and Kwame Nkrumah's innovations are most remembered for their effects.

DOMINANT POSITION

Early in the nineteenth century, British imperial policies started to slacken in response to calls for more self-determination, first coming largely from the inhabitants of the most developed colonies who were of British ancestry. In the 1840s, Canada became the first country to have self-government. It was also the first dominion (1867). The relationship between a colony and an imperial state was profoundly altered by dominion status, which permitted self-government and substantial freedom in international affairs. When visiting Adelaide, Australia, in 1884, British statesman Lord Rosebery described the empire as "a Commonwealth of countries."

When Australia's states amalgamated as the Commonwealth of Australia in 1901, it attained dominion status. South Africa, New Zealand, and the Irish Free State followed in 1907, 1910, and 1921, respectively. India and the five dominions each had a representative in the League of Nations, which was the precursor of the UN.

The British Empire's dominions and Great Britain were described as "autonomous communities within the British Empire, equal in status, in no way subordinate one to another in any aspect of their domestic or external affairs, though united by a common allegiance to the Crown, and freely associated as members of the British Commonwealth of Nations" in the Balfour Report of 1926.

The de facto independence of the dominions was recognized legally when the Statute of Westminster was enacted by the UK parliament in 1931. The Act was rapidly enacted by the parliaments of Canada, South Africa, and the Irish Free State. It was embraced by Australia in 1942 and by New Zealand in 1947. In 1949, Newfoundland gave up its sovereign status and became a part of Canada.

Republican Participation

The fight for self-government was also becoming more intense in India, which at the time also included Bangladesh and Pakistan. In 1947, Sri Lanka, along with India and Pakistan, became independent as dominions and Commonwealth members. As the first Commonwealth nations where the demand for independence stemmed from native people rather than communities derived mostly from British immigrants, these events signaled a shift in the course of the organization. The foundation for the development of a multiracial Commonwealth was thus set.

The Commonwealth then faced a dilemma over its constitution. The assumption was that the association's main tenet would be that each member would have the British monarch as their head of state. The Indian Constituent Assembly chose a republican system of administration but expressed a desire to be a part of the Commonwealth. India might continue to be a member of the Commonwealth as a republic, but it was decided to accept the monarch "as the emblem of the free association of independent member states and as such Head of the Commonwealth" during the 1949 Commonwealth Prime Ministers Meeting.

This achievement paved the possibility for additional nations to join the Commonwealth that possessed republican constitutions or sovereign monarchies. 37 of the 53 members did not recognize Queen Elizabeth II as their official head of state at the beginning of 2006, but they all recognized her as the head of the Commonwealth.

Additionally, the Queen serves as the head of state for 16 sovereign Commonwealth nations. She is the governor of each of these states separately. With the exception of the United Kingdom, the nations over which the Queen reigns are now officially referred to as realms (though the name is practically defunct in reality). A governor-general serves as the Queen's representative and holds the formal positions of head of state.

Blowing the Wind

As the first African nation with a majority government, the Gold Coast in West Africa joined the Commonwealth in 1957 after gaining independence as the Republic of Ghana. This was the beginning of what British Prime Minister Harold Macmillan referred to as "the wind of revolution blowing over Africa." The UK lost control of various regions of Africa, Asia, the Caribbean, the Mediterranean, and the Pacific during the course of the next two decades. The number of Commonwealth members grew quickly.

Following Nigeria and Cyprus (1960), Sierra Leone and Tanzania (1961), Jamaica, Trinidad and Tobago, and Uganda (1962), Malaya (later integrated into Malaysia) also gained independence in 1957. Most nations that gained independence decided to join the Commonwealth. Following the 1994 elections, South Africa was re-admitted, bringing the total number of members to 51. Mozambique, which had long expressed a desire to join the organization and had been associated with it during the protracted Southern African battle for racial equality, was granted membership in November 1995. Cameroon, which has been sovereign since 1960, joined in October 1995.

A few nations declined to sign on. Ireland left in 1949, and Myanmar (formerly Burma; Independent 1947) made the decision not to join. Several former UK protectorates, mandates, protectorates, or protected nations, mostly in the Middle East, made the decision not to join the Commonwealth after gaining independence. The Maldives gained their independence in 1965, but they didn't join the group until 1982. Samoa, which had previously been a UN Trust Territory run by New Zealand, gained independence in 1962 but did not accredit until 1970.

Three nations left the Commonwealth before returning. After other members recognized Bangladesh as a distinct state (which had previously been a part of Pakistan), Pakistan withdrew from the organization in 1972, but was warmly welcomed back in 1989 when the democratically elected government requested to rejoin.

In 1961, South Africa's membership became inactive. It was necessary to submit a formal reapplication for membership once it became a republic. This was made evident by the Commonwealth's opposition to the government's at-the-time apartheid policies, and South Africa resigned as a result. South Africa was welcomed back into the organization on June 1st, 1994, after the democratic elections of that year.

After a military takeover and the formation of a republic in 1987, Fiji Islands' membership was terminated since it, too, garnered no support from other members to reapply. In October 1997, the nation rejoined after a ten-year absence and the start of a constitutional reform process.

Nigeria, a participant in many significant projects since its independence in 1960 and a member of the Commonwealth, was expelled in November 1995 after Heads of Government determined that it had broken the ideals of the 1991 Harare Declaration. The first suspension period was two years. Beginning in 1995, the Commonwealth Ministerial Action Group kept an eye on events in Nigeria (as well as The Gambia and Sierra Leone). With the appointment of a new head of state in the middle of 1998, Nigeria started a transitional path toward a civilian democracy. With the swearing-in of a democratically elected civilian president on May 29, 1999, the country's exclusion from the Commonwealth was revoked after it finished its election schedule in early 1999.

In recent years, three members—Fiji Islands, Pakistan, and Zimbabwe—have all had their membership in the association's councils suspended until the restoration of democracy in conformity with the constitution. In December 2001, the ban for the Fiji Islands was removed. The Zimbabwean government left the Commonwealth after the CHOGM Statement on Zimbabwe in December 2003. In May 2004, Pakistan's ban was removed.

GROUP OF EMINENT PEOPLE IN THE COMMONWEALTH

The Eminent Persons Group (EPG), which was reinstated in 2009, is a group of eminent people who serve as an acknowledged advisory body to and on behalf of the Commonwealth. To "undertake an analysis of alternatives for change in order to bring the different institutions of the Commonwealth into a stronger and more effective framework of co-operation and partnership," according to the EPG's mission statement.

With its report, "A Commonwealth of the People: Time for Urgent Reform," the EPG most recently carried out its responsibility to advise on possible reform within the Commonwealth at CHOGM 2011 in Perth, Australia. In order to make the Commonwealth relevant in the context of current affairs, the report reflected a desire to re-establish the Commonwealth's identity, with a focus on issues relating to human, political, and civil rights as well as development, trade, and investment, as well as environmental concerns.

The EPG is led by Tun Abdullah Ahmad Badawi of Malaysia. Other members include Dr. Emmanuel Akwetey of Ghana, Ms. Patricia Francis of Jamaica, Dr. Asma Jahangir of Pakistan, Mr. Samuel Kavuma of Uganda and the Commonwealth Youth Caucus, Senator Hugh Segal of Canada, The Hon. Michael Kirby of Australia, Rt. Hon. Sir Malcolm Rifkind of the United Kingdom, Sir Ronald Sanders of Guyana, and Sir Ieremia (Kiribati).

1. Tun Abdullah Ahmad Badawi was Malaysia's first deputy prime minister and served as minister of finance, education, defense, foreign policy, and home affairs. In 2003, he replaced Mahathir Mohamad as prime minister and set about creating a modern, progressive, and multiracial society while also advocating for extensive change. He was a founder of the Commonwealth Youth Program and a member of the Commonwealth Ministerial Action Group.

2. The founding Executive Director of the Institute of Democratic Governance (IDEG) in Ghana is Dr. Emmanuel O. Akwetey. He supports human development and democratic government. The Government of Ghana, the African Capacity Building Foundation (ACBF), the Government of Liberia, UNDP, and a number of bilateral donor organizations have also sought his advice.

3. The International Trade Centre in Geneva is led by Ms. Patricia R. Francis. Her most recent position was as president of Jamaica Trade and Invest, where she had been in that position since 1995. She presided over the World Association of Investment Promotion Agencies twice, served as head of the China Caribbean Business Council and the Organization for Economic Co-operation and Development's Caribbean Rim Investment Initiative.

4. A well-known Pakistani human rights activist is Dr. Asma Jilani Jahangir. She served as President of the Pakistan Supreme Court Bar Association and Chair of the Human Rights Commission of Pakistan. She has two special rapporteur positions at the UN: one on the freedom of religion or belief and the other on extrajudicial, summary, or arbitrary execution.

5. Mr. Samuel Kavuma serves as the Commonwealth Youth Caucus' temporary chair. Since 1997, he has served as a student leader in Uganda. He was chosen to serve on Uganda's National Youth Council in 2004. In 2007, he was chosen to represent the Regional Youth Caucus. He also played a key role in the creation of UN-one-stop Habitat's youth center.

5. The Hon. Michael Kirby AC CMG served as a judge on the Australian High Court (1996–2009). He served as the International Commission of Jurists' President (1995–1998), and he shared the Gruber Justice Prize in 2010.

6. From 1979 until 1997, Sir Malcolm Rifkind, KCMG, QC, was a minister in the British government, first as the secretary of state for defense and later as the foreign secretary. He presently serves as a member of parliament and as chair of the committee that oversees the intelligence agencies of the UK.

7. Sir Ronald Sanders KCMG is a former Caribbean diplomat, author, and international consultant who have worked as a trade negotiator and on Commonwealth advisory committees. He has held important roles in both the public and business sectors, including serving on the UNESCO Executive Board. He's written a lot on tiny states.

8. Senator Hugh Segal CM was elected to the Canadian Senate in 2005. He has chaired the committees overseeing foreign affairs and counterterrorism. He worked as the

Prime Minister of Canada's Chief of Staff, Ontario's Associate Cabinet Secretary for Federal-Provincial Affairs and Policies and Priorities, and the Leader of the Opposition's Legislative Assistant (Ottawa). He oversaw the independent Institute for Research on Public Policy as its president.

9. Sir Ieremia Tabai is a current member of the Kiribatian parliament. He served as the first President of the nation from 1979 until 1991, when he resigned in accordance with the legislation after a maximum of three terms, or twelve years, in office. Both Kiribati and New Zealand provided Sir Ieremia with his education. He attended St Andrews College in Christchurch for three years before transferring to Victoria University in Wellington to complete a degree in business

Chapter three

MEMBERS OF THE COMMONWEALTH

The Commonwealth is a voluntary association of 56 independent and equal countries. Its roots go back to the British Empire, but membership of the modern Commonwealth does not depend on formerly being part of the British Empire.

ELIGIBILITY CRITERIA FOR MEMBERSHIP

At the Commonwealth Heads of Government Meeting in Uganda in November 2007, Heads of Government reviewed the recommendations of the Committee on Commonwealth Membership and agreed on the following core criteria for Membership:

- ✔ an applicant country should, as a general rule, have had a historic constitutional association with an existing Commonwealth member, save in exceptional circumstances

- ✔ in exceptional circumstances, applications should be considered on a case-by-case basis

✔   an applicant country should accept and comply with Commonwealth fundamental values, principles, and priorities as set out in the 1971 Declaration of Commonwealth Principles and contained in other subsequent Declarations

✔   an applicant country must demonstrate commitment to: democracy and democratic processes, including free and fair elections and representative legislatures; the rule of law and independence of the judiciary; good governance, including a well-trained public service and transparent public accounts; and protection of human rights, freedom of expression, and equality of opportunity

✔   an applicant country should accept Commonwealth norms and conventions, such as the use of the English language as the medium of inter-Commonwealth relations, and acknowledge Queen Elizabeth II as the Head of the Commonwealth

✔   new members should be encouraged to join the Commonwealth Foundation, and to promote vigorous civil society and business organizations within their countries, and to foster participatory democracy through regular civil society consultations.

Heads of Government also agreed that, where an existing member changes its formal constitutional status, it should not have to reapply for Commonwealth membership provided that it continues to meet all the criteria for membership.

Heads endorsed the other recommendations of the Committee, including a four-step process for considering applications for membership; new members being required to augment the existing budget of the Secretariat; and countries in accumulated arrears being renamed 'Members in Arrears'. They also agreed with the Committee's recommendations on Overseas Territories, Special Guests and strategic partnerships.

PROCESS FOR JOINING THE COMMONWEALTH

For eligible countries, there is a membership process which has to be followed once the formal expression of interest to join is triggered. This entails the following:

1. An informal assessment undertaken by the Secretary-General following an expression of interest by an aspirant country

2. Consultation by the Secretary-General with member states

3. An invitation to the interested country to make a formal application

4. A formal application presenting evidence of the functioning of democratic processes and popular support in that country for joining the Commonwealth.

The procedure also sets out that the application would thereafter be considered by Heads of Government at the next CHOGM and, if they reach consensus on accepting it, that country would then join the Commonwealth and be invited to attend subsequent meetings.

REJOINING THE COMMONWEALTH

A Commonwealth member state that has withdrawn or was expelled from the Commonwealth would need to reapply for membership. Although Commonwealth Heads have not set out any re-joining criteria, it is expected that a country would demonstrate that it continues to uphold the principles and values of the Commonwealth that it espoused when it first joined.

List of members of the Commonwealth of Nations by date joined

COUNTRY	COMMENCEMENT	POPULATION	AREA
Antigua and Barbuda	1981	10M	440km²
Australia	1931	25.74M	741000km²
Bahamas	1973	0.40M	4000km²
Bangledesh	1972	166,30M	148000km²
Barbados	1966	0.29M	430km²
Belize	1981	0.40M	23000km²
Botswana	1966	2.40M	582000km²
Brunei	1984	0.44M	770km²
Cameroon	1995	27.22M	75000km²
Canada	1931	38.25M	9985000km²
Cyprus	1961	1.22M	9250km²

Dominica	1978	0.07M	750km²
Eswatini	1968	1.17M	17000km²
Gambia	1965	2.49M	11000km²
Ghana	1957	31.73M	239000km²
Grenada	1974	0.11M	340km²
Guyana	1966	0.79M	215000km²
India	1947	1.3B	3287000km²
Jamaica	1962	2.97M	11000km²
Kenya	1963	54.99M	580000km²
Kiribati	1979	0.12M	810km²
Lesotho	1966	2.16M	30000km²
Malawi	1964	19.65M	118000km²
Malaysia	1957	32.78M	330000km²
Malta	1964	0.52M	320km²
Mauritius	1968	1.27M	2040km²
Mozambique	1995	32.16M	786000km²
Namibia	1990	2.59M	824000km²
Nauru	1999	0.01M	21km²
New Zealand	1931	5.12M	268000km²

Nigeria	1960	217.40M	924000km²
Pakistan	1947	225.20M	796000km²
Papua new guinea	1975	9.12M	463000km²
Rwanda	2009	13.28M	26000km²
Saint kitts and Nevis	1983	0.05M	260km²
Saint Lucia	1979	0.18M	620km²
Saint vicent and Grenadines	1979	0.11M	390km²
Samoa	1970	0.20M	2840km²
Seychelles	1976	0.10M	460km²
Sierraleone	1961	8.18M	72000km²
Singapore	1965	5.45M	719km²
Solomon island	1978	0.70M	29000km²
South Africa	1931	60.04M	1219000km²
Sri lanka	1948	22.16M	66000km²
Tanzania	1961	61.50M	947000km²
Tonga	1970	0.11M	750km²
Trinidad and Tobago	1962	1.40M	5130km²
Tuvalu	1978	0.01M	26km²

Uganda	1962	47.12M	242000km²
United kingdom	1931	67,33M	244000km²
Vanuatu	1980	0.31M	12000km²
Zambia	1964	18.92M	753000km²

WorldData.info

FORMER MEMBER COUNTRIES

COUNTRY	**EXIT**	**POPULATION**	**AREA**
Fiji	2009	0.90M	18000km²
Ireland	1949	5.03M	70000km²
Maldives	2016	0.54M	300km²
Zimbabwe	2003	15.09M	391000km²

WorldData.info

AUSTRALIA IN THE COMMONWEALTH

Australia is a founding member of the modern Commonwealth and has been an active participant in Commonwealth organizations, programs and meetings for over 60 years. It is the third-largest contributor to the Commonwealth budget. Australia currently serves as Vice-Chair of the Commonwealth Ministerial Action Group (CMAG), and is represented by Australia's Foreign Minister.

As Commonwealth Chair-in-Office from 2011-2013, Australia played a leading role in the development of the Commonwealth Charter. Australia is represented on the Commonwealth Secretariat's Board of Governors, and its Executive Committee, by the Australian High Commissioner to the United Kingdom.

Australia supports the Commonwealth to promote human rights, democratic norms and good governance among member countries. The Commonwealth's work in supporting inclusive growth and sustainable development also recognises the intrinsic connection between the security and stability of governments and economic development.

NIGERIA IN THE COMMONWEALTH

When Nigeria gained political independence in 1960, it officially joined the Commonwealth and has been a participating member ever since. The lone exception was when Nigeria was expelled from the organization due to human rights violations and the extrajudicial death of the Ogoni 9 headed by Ken Saro Wiwa in 1995. This occurred from November 11, 1995 and May 29, 1999.

The Commonwealth's visa-free entrance policy was one of the perks of Nigeria's membership when it was established in 1960. This made it much easier for organization members to move about, do business, engage in sports, share ideas, and communicate with one another. The visa-free policy, however, came to an end in the late 1980s as a result of an unsustainable increase in the pace of migration from underdeveloped to industrialized nations. During that time, academics, professionals, and even unskilled laborers started to flee to the developed Commonwealth nations, particularly the United Kingdom, Canada, Australia, New Zealand, and Malta, since Nigeria was being brutally mishandled by military dictatorships.

Even while that window has closed, exchanges in education, sports, and culture have persisted, although in scaled back ways. There is still a lot of excitement around the Commonwealth Games. Thousands of Nigerians have benefited from Commonwealth Scholarships to destinations including the United Kingdom, Scotland, Canada, Australia, India, New Zealand, and many more, and these exchanges between Commonwealths nations continue.

Although the Commonwealth has received various criticisms, including that it is a colonial holdover from the defunct British Empire, a constant reminder of the British dominance over other countries and peoples, and a largely inactive organization that serves as a mere talking shop for world leaders without any real power or influence, its supporters view the organization as a success story for the ways it has promoted the ideals of democracy, human rights, and the rule of law. The line of potential members is another example cited by those who support it as proof of its vitality and ongoing importance. It is known that numerous nations with no connections to the Commonwealth have applied for membership in the group. Many of its tiny and impoverished members, who make up the bulk of its membership, are able to network and form strategic alliances in the competitive contemporary world, which some claim is its primary attraction.

Since 2013, the Commonwealth has been looking at methods to revive the visa-free policy among its members, boost commerce, and potentially establish a free trade zone inside the Commonwealth. In the UK, where many politicians and Euro skeptics publicly support the Commonwealth free trade zone as an alternative to the UK's membership in the European Union, the topic of trade, particularly the free trade zone, has acquired more traction. They may readily recall the period between 1940 and 1970, when more than half of all UK commerce was with Commonwealth nations.

SOUTH AFRICA IN THE COMMONWEALTH

Since 1917, the Commonwealth has had a long-standing relationship with the Republic of South Africa (SA). The British Empire changed throughout the 19th century, when its imperial power was softer, giving rise to the notions of the Commonwealth. The phrase "Commonwealth of Nations" was created when several British colonies obtained dominion status, which allowed them substantial freedom in foreign affairs and self-government, changing the way those colonies interacted with the British Empire.

The Commonwealth kept up with technological advancements around the start of the century. The 2002 Coolum Declaration on the Commonwealth in the 21st Century and the 2003 Aso Rock Declaration on Development and Democracy were significant pronouncements in this respect. The decision to form an Eminent Persons Group (EPG), a proposal for the creation of the Commonwealth Partnership Platform Portal

(CP3), the creation of a "Good Offices for the Environment" role for the Secretary-General, and a review of the mandate and working methodology are all outcomes of the biennial Commonwealth Heads of Government Meeting (CHOGM), which was held in Port of Spain in 2009.

According to the Statute of Westminster, South Africa joined the Commonwealth in 1931. The Commonwealth's opposition to the systems of apartheid led to SA's expulsion in 1961. The group was crucial in pushing for the abolition of institutionalized racism during the anti-apartheid movement. The Gleneagles Agreement, which forbade sports contests with South Africa, was endorsed by the leaders of the Commonwealth in unanimity in 1977. Through the Kuala Lumpur Statement, the group expanded its campaign against racism in South Africa in 1989. These choices made by the organization undoubtedly helped the apartheid Government come under increasing international criticism.

Thus, notwithstanding South Africa's exclusion from the Commonwealth, it is important to recognize the association's contribution to the worldwide effort to isolate the minority Government. As former President Thabo Mbeki stated, "this community of countries painstakingly brought immense pressure worldwide, in many different ways to bear on the racist and authoritarian regime," the Commonwealth's involvement throughout these years is expressly acknowledged by the present Government. In light of this, it is possible to see this legacy of support as a key factor in SA's choice to rejoin the Commonwealth once the first democratic government was elected in 1994.

Since entering the Commonwealth again, SA has taken an active role in the association's numerous governing bodies and ministerial gatherings. SA also serves on the Board of Governors of the Commonwealth of Learning (COL) and is one of the largest volunteer funders of the organization. In addition, South Africa grants Commonwealth Scholarship and Fellowship Plan scholarships and fellowships to nationals of participating nations. The Secretariat of the Commonwealth Council for Educational Administration and Management is also located in South Africa.

Through a number of development initiatives sponsored by the Commonwealth, SA has also profited from participation in the alliance. These include the creation of the tourism growth strategy for the Mpumalanga province in 2007–2008, the benchmarking of the fruit export trade logistics chain in South Africa in 2007–2008, the hiring of an e-learning and website designer/developer in 2005–2006, a study tour to India by the Agricultural Research Council (ARC) of South Africa in 2004, and the hiring of an advisor to the Commission for Gender Equality in 1999. The Commonwealth fulfills its development purpose by supporting such projects, demonstrating its worth as a multinational organization.

The Commonwealth - early and modern developments

The concepts of the Commonwealth have its roots in the 19th century, stemming from the transformation of the British Empire with the softening of its imperial rule. The term "Commonwealth of Nations" was coined when some British colonies acquired dominion status, which allowed self-Government and extensive independence in foreign affairs, thereby reshaping the relationship with the British Empire. However, the defining moment arrived in 1931, when the Balfour Report of 1926 was incorporated into British Law as the Statute of Westminster, giving legal recognition to the de facto independence of the Dominions.

The birth of the modern Commonwealth is symbolised by the London declaration of 1949, which led to a revision of the criteria for membership. These revisions allowed India to remain a member of the association as a republic and paved the way for newly independent countries to become members of the Commonwealth. As British rule ended in many parts of Africa, Asia, the Caribbean, the Mediterranean and Pacific, the Commonwealth became the natural association of choice, as the vast majority of newly independent states chose to join the association, thereby rapidly expanding the membership.

The Commonwealth in the 21st Century and beyond

At the turn of the century, the Commonwealth continued to adapt to the changing times. Key declarations in this regard were the 2002 Coolum Declaration on the Commonwealth in the 21st Century and the 2003 Aso Rock Declaration on Development and Democracy. Emanating from the biennial gathering of the Commonwealth Heads of Government Meeting (CHOGM), held in the Port of Spain in 2009, was as a decision to form an Eminent Persons Group (EPG), a proposal for the development of the Commonwealth Partnership Platform Portal (CP3), the creation of a "Good Offices for the Environment" role for the Secretary-General and a review of the mandate and working methodology.

It is evident that over the years the Commonwealth has deepened its mandate. Today, the work of the Commonwealth covers a wide range of cross-cutting issues, ranging from those dealing with democracy, economics, education, gender, governance, human rights, law, small states, sport, sustainability, and youth. In order to fulfil its mandate and deliver its programmes, the association provides assistance to its members in the form of policy development, technical assistance and advisory services. The work of the association is carried out through the three intergovernmental organisations (The Secretariat, The Commonwealth Foundation and The Commonwealth of Learning) and specialised Sub-Committees which operate at an international, regional, national and community level. In fulfilling its duties, the Commonwealth further collaborates with other international organisations such as the United Nations (UN) and in partnerships such as the G20.

By reinforcing its principles, reaffirming its core values, deepening its mandates and widening its membership, the Commonwealth has attempted to adapt to the changing times to ensure its relevance and effectiveness in the 21st century. Credit can certainly be given for the strides made by the association in this regard. The adaptation of the association to the changing times has by no means ended as it continues to review its action plans and the structure of its various institutions.

These plans will take shape when the Commonwealth convenes the CHOGM in Perth in October 2011. However, whilst the association has developed and continues to develop an ambitious mandate, a true measure of its effectiveness and relevance can only be determined objectively by analysing the benefits to its members. This paper now examines the relationship between SA and the Commonwealth and investigates why the country remains a member of this association.

Withdrawal of South Africa from the commonwealth

According to the Statute of Westminster, South Africa joined the Commonwealth in 1931. The Commonwealth's opposition to the systems of apartheid led to SA's expulsion in 1961. The group was crucial in pushing for the abolition of institutionalized racism during the anti-apartheid movement. The Gleneagles Agreement, which forbade sports contests with South Africa, was endorsed by the leaders of the Commonwealth in unanimity in 1977. Through the Kuala Lumpur Statement, the group expanded its campaign against racism in South Africa in 1989. These choices made by the organization undoubtedly helped the apartheid Government come under increasing international criticism.

Thus, notwithstanding South Africa's exclusion from the Commonwealth, it is important to recognize the association's contribution to the worldwide effort to isolate the minority Government. As former President Thabo Mbeki stated, "this community of countries painstakingly brought immense pressure worldwide, in many different ways to bear on the racist and authoritarian regime," the Commonwealth's involvement throughout these years is expressly acknowledged by the present Government. In light of this, it is possible to see this legacy of support as a key factor in SA's choice to rejoin the Commonwealth once the first democratic government was elected in 1994.

Since entering the Commonwealth again, SA has taken an active role in the association's numerous governing bodies and ministerial gatherings. SA also serves on the Board of Governors of the Commonwealth of Learning (COL) and is one of the largest volunteer funders of the organization. In addition, South Africa grants Commonwealth Scholarship and Fellowship Plan scholarships and fellowships to nationals of participating nations. The Secretariat of the Commonwealth Council for Educational Administration and Management is also located in South Africa.

In addition, SA has hosted four Commonwealth gatherings since 1994, including the CHOGM annual summit in 1999. As president, directors, and vice chairs of the different Commonwealth organizations, a number of South Africans have also held important roles in the Commonwealth. Therefore, the nation's resources and financial obligations to the Commonwealth are an indication of the importance it has placed on this affiliation.

Through a number of development initiatives sponsored by the Commonwealth, SA has also profited from participation in the alliance. These include the creation of the tourism growth strategy for the Mpumalanga province in 2007–2008, the benchmarking of the fruit export trade logistics chain in South Africa in 2007–2008, the hiring of an e-learning and website designer/developer in 2005–2006, a study tour to India by the Agricultural Research Council (ARC) of South Africa in 2004, and the hiring of an advisor to the Commission for Gender Equality in 1999. The Commonwealth fulfills its development purpose by supporting such projects, demonstrating its worth as a multinational organization.

Overall, even if the Commonwealth has effectively aided South Africa's growth, it would seem that SA's contribution to the Commonwealth surpasses the advantages of association membership. Such a judgment, nonetheless, is hasty since it simply takes the association's resource and financial aspects into account. One must go deeper in order to answer the issues raised at the beginning of this piece, particularly why SA continues to be a member of the organization. This will be accomplished by going back to where SA's international relations and foreign policy first began.

SA FOREIGN POLICY AND THE COMMONWEALTH

The State of the Nation Addresses, Budget Vote Speeches, Addresses to International and Regional Bodies, and numerous Foreign Policy Discussion Documents all contribute to the multifaceted mix of policies, principles, goals, strategies, and plans that make up SA's foreign policy. These values include a dedication to human rights, democracy, justice and international law, peace, the African Agenda, and economic growth, according the Department of International Relations and Cooperation's (DIRCO) 2010-2013 Strategic Plan. The Commonwealth subscribes to many of these ideals. Therefore, SA and the Commonwealth are united by these common values and beliefs. Given the parallels between SA's national interests and those of the association, one may argue that the Commonwealth is a natural association for the country.

The association's activities and programs of action are mostly focused on solving problems that are consistent with SA's national goals. Accordingly, SA and the Commonwealth see some of the most important issues facing the world today as capacity building, economic and social development, eliminating living standard gaps, and reducing poverty and illiteracy.

The United Nations Millennium Development Goals (MDGs) and the New Partnership for Africa's Development are two of the most essential concerns that South Africa firmly supports, and the Commonwealth's programs are cross-cutting and address both of these issues (NEPAD). To this aim, SA has often contributed to discussions at different Commonwealth gatherings on topics pertaining to the MDGs, the African Agenda, and NEPAD. Additionally, SA has pushed for strong stances on the three most important issues of the last ten years: terrorism, trade liberalization, and climate change.

Now it is clear that there are no hidden parallels between the national interests of SA and the Commonwealth's goal. As stated in the DIRCO Strategic Plan, SA favors multilateral diplomacy as one of the ways to advance its foreign policy since it recognizes the value of collaboration in the age of globalization. Due to the variety of its members, belonging to the Commonwealth not only provides a platform in this respect but also a point of contact for North-South and South-South Cooperation. The fundamental justification for South Africa's participation in the organization in the twenty-first century, despite the concept of historical loyalty being obvious, is the similarity between the nation's norms, values, and interests and those of the Commonwealth. By encouraging cooperation, the shared values, beliefs, and interests bring people together and build a positive work atmosphere. This essay thus holds the opinion that SA should continue to be a member of this organization.

CANADA IN THE COMMONWEALTH

Canada became a member of the British Commonwealth for the first time in 1931. Canada has been a key player in the development of the modern Commonwealth since the London Declaration in 1949.

Throughout her 70-year reign, Queen Elizabeth II presided as the Commonwealth's head of state. King Charles III, who attended the Commonwealth Heads of Government Meeting in Kigali, Rwanda, in June 2022, is now in the position of Head.

From 1965 until 1975, Canadian diplomat Arnold Smith served as the first secretary-general of the Commonwealth. Patricia Scotland, the current secretary-general, is the first woman to occupy the position and the sixth secretary-general of the Commonwealth. Canada twice hosted the CHOGM, in 1973 and 1987.

Canada had a particular interest in the Commonwealth since it was one of the countries that helped to establish it in the early 1930s. After World War II, the majority of the former British colonies gained their independence, a move that was generally supported by Canadians. Many of these nations then sought to join the Commonwealth. Some of the newly independent countries, like India, were republics, which presented the question of whether a republic could be a member of an organization tied to a common monarch. Suddenly, the Commonwealth was regarded as a group that would, like the empire, use its authority to transcend racial and cultural divides. The Commonwealth's members decided that republics might join if they chose to recognize the sovereign as the organization's "leader." Canadians, who belong to a republican hemisphere, naturally embraced the new organizational idea since they saw Canada as a middleman between the former Commonwealth members and the newly developed nations.

The Suez Crisis, a significant strain on both the Commonwealth and global peace, demonstrated Canada's capacity to serve as an intermediate within the Commonwealth. Australia and New Zealand, for instance, were inclined to share the United Kingdom's strategic concerns, but India was horrified and incensed by what it saw as a coordinated act of aggression. Lester Pearson's Canada was able to mediate between the United Kingdom and India, allowing both sides to maintain their dignity and safeguarding the Commonwealth's unity.

Canada too acted as an uninterested friend throughout the turmoil that was brought on by South Africa's apartheid regime. South Africa was not simply an outlier but also a disgrace to a multiethnic organization like the Commonwealth. However, the Commonwealth's fundamental tenet was noninterference in the private matters of its members. When certain nations pushed to have South Africa ejected from the Commonwealth Conference in 1960, the problem reached a head. The UK, Australia, and New Zealand condemned this transgression of the nonintervention principle. Once again attempting to act as an objective mediator, Canada ultimately decided to vote for expulsion. Although its actions sometimes caused friction with the United Kingdom, Canada typically backed the goals of non-white member nations within the Commonwealth (for example, it approved economic penalties against the white minority rule in Rhodesia [now Zimbabwe]).

The United Kingdom started thinking about joining the European Common Market in the early 1960s. Canada vehemently opposed Britain's accession because of concern that it would imply the diminishment of the imperial advantages that, since 1932, had provided the Commonwealth with a material as well as an emotional foundation. However, when Britain ultimately joined in 1973, Canada, which was then governed by a liberal government, had already accepted Britain's choice and was concentrating on doing everything it could to increase Canadian commerce with the Common Market. But with Britain's admission, the Commonwealth would become less and less about links to the tangible world and more and more about feeling and tradition.

Some nations have left the Commonwealth or have been suspended.

Three nations that have previously left the Commonwealth have subsequently rejoined. When it became evident that its reapplication for membership after becoming a republic would be denied, South Africa withdrew in 1961. South Africa was welcomed back into the association after the democratic elections in 1994.

After other members recognized Bangladesh in 1972, Pakistan departed and then rejoined after the democratic elections of 1989.

But when the democratically elected government was overthrown in October 1999, the nation was expelled from the Commonwealth Councils until democracy had been restored. After a meeting of the Commonwealth Ministerial Action Group (CMAG) in Kampala, this suspension was withdrawn in May 2004 but reinstated in November 2007 in anticipation of the return of democracy and the rule of law. On May 12, 2008, CMAG convened once again and determined that Pakistan's government had made progress toward meeting its commitments in line with Commonwealth core values and principles. As a result, it resolved to reinstate Pakistan in the Commonwealth councils.

After a military coup imposed a constitution that was against Commonwealth values in 1987, the Fiji Islands' membership expired. It was reinstated in October 1997 after it had started a constitutional reform process. After the democratically elected government was overthrown in May 2000, the nation was expelled from the Commonwealth Councils. Suspension was removed in December 2001 once democracy and the rule of law were restored in line with the constitution, but it was reinstated in December 2006 after the military once again overthrew the democratically elected government. As agreed upon both the Pacific Islands Forum and the interim government of Fiji, elections must be conducted by the date of March 2009, CMAG said once again in May 2008. However, no elections were held, and CMAG later regretted that Fiji continued to go against the norms and objectives of the Commonwealth.

The apparent abrogation of Fiji's constitution and the further solidification of authoritarian leadership, according to CMAG, led to a dramatic worsening of the country's condition by the end of July 2009. Additionally, it voiced severe worry about the regime's plans to put off a return to democracy for another five years. On September 1, 2009, Fiji was permanently expelled from the Commonwealth. Nigeria was the first nation to have its membership suspended in this manner, back in 1995. Despite this, the Commonwealth Secretariat has continued to work with the Fiji Islands to encourage and advance inclusive political discussion and the restoration of constitutional democracy.

No nation has ever been officially ejected from the Commonwealth, but in November 1995, the Heads of Government of the Commonwealth took the at the time unprecedented action of suspending the membership of one of its members—Nigeria. When a democratically elected civilian president was sworn into office on May 29, 1999, this suspension was overturned.

Following the March 2002 presidential election, which was marred by a high level of politically motivated violence and during which the conditions did not adequately allow for a free expression of the electors' will, Zimbabwe, which had been a member since its independence in April 1980, was suspended from Commonwealth councils. The Zimbabwean government then left the Commonwealth in December 2003 as a result of the CHOGM Statement on Zimbabwe.

The Gambia's government announced its exit from the Commonwealth on state television on October 3, 2013, and Commonwealth Secretary-General Kamalesh Sharma acknowledged the withdrawal on October 4.

Chapter four

The British monarch's role in the Commonwealth

The British Commonwealth included eight nations by 1949, each of which was ruled by King George VI. India, however, wanted to become a republic but did not want to do it by leaving the Commonwealth. India became a republic in 1950, and this was made possible by the introduction of the title Head of the Commonwealth for the King. Later, other countries such as Pakistan, Sri Lanka, Ghana, and Singapore also established themselves as republics while still recognizing the British monarch as the Commonwealth's Head of State.

The United Kingdom, Canada, Australia, New Zealand, South Africa, India, Pakistan, and Ceylon were all ruled by King George VI at the time, together with Canada, Australia, New Zealand, South Africa, and Australia. The Indian Cabinet wanted the nation to become a republic, but did not want it to leave the Commonwealth once George VI was no longer king, as occurred to Ireland. In order to address this, the London Declaration, drafted by the Canadian Prime Minister Louis St. Laurent and released in late April 1949, declared that the King was the head of the Commonwealth and served as a symbol of the free association of Commonwealth nations. On January 26, 1950, India approved a republican constitution, making Rajendra Prasad its new head of state. However, George VI was still regarded as the head of the Commonwealth.

When Elizabeth II ascended to the throne in 1952, she said at the time, "The Empires of the Past have no relation to the Commonwealth. It's a brand-new idea founded on the noblest aspects of the human spirit, including friendship, loyalty, and the yearning for freedom and peace." The word "Head of the Commonwealth" was first added to the monarch's titles the following year when each of the Commonwealth nations enacted a Royal Style and Titles Act.

In order to represent herself as Head of the Commonwealth without being connected to her position as the monarch of any specific nation, the Queen had a personal flag made in December 1960. When the Queen traveled to Commonwealth nations where she was head of state but did not have a royal standard for that nation or when she was not head of state, as well as during Commonwealth-related ceremonies in the UK, the flag eventually took the place of the British Royal Standard.

Along with the Commonwealth Secretary General and Commonwealth Chair-in-Office, the Head of the Commonwealth is regarded by the other members of the Commonwealth of Nations as the "symbol of their free association" and acts as a leader. Queen Elizabeth II served as the head of state of 15 Commonwealth members, but since she was also the head of the Commonwealth, she had no authority over the administration of any Commonwealth state. The Queen maintained communication with the Secretariat, the Commonwealth's main administrative body, as well as the Secretary General of the Commonwealth, in order to stay up to date on developments within the Commonwealth.

The biannual Commonwealth Heads of Government Meeting (CHOGM), which takes place in several Commonwealth nations, is attended by the leader of the Commonwealth or a delegate. On the recommendation of Canadian Prime Minister Pierre Trudeau in 1973, when the CHOGM was first held in Canada, the queen started this custom. The leader of the Commonwealth attends a CHOGM reception and supper, meets privately with the leaders of Commonwealth nations, and delivers a keynote address during the summit.

The Commonwealth Games are held every four years, and the head of the Commonwealth or a representative has attended. Prior to the start of the Commonwealth Games, the Queen's Baton Relay was conducted, sending a message to all Commonwealth nations and territories. At her coronation, Queen Elizabeth observed a feeling of a new Commonwealth. The Commonwealth, she said, "bears little similarity to the ancient empires. It's a brand-new idea founded on the noblest aspects of the human spirit, including friendship, loyalty, and the yearning for freedom and peace.

By establishing tradition, the Queen's job today encompasses a variety of symbolic duties that strengthen the Commonwealth link and the feeling of family. At Heads of Government Meetings, in country capitals around the Commonwealth, and in London, she has conversations with top officials. During each summit, she travels to the host nation and meets the leaders in person and in bigger formal gatherings.

During her state trips, she has met with leaders and ordinary citizens in the majority of Commonwealth nations, not only those where she is the head of state. She gives a broadcast on Commonwealth Day and attends other celebrations, such as the multifaith service, which is customarily held at Westminster Abbey, and the Commonwealth Secretary-reception. General's

The leaders of the Commonwealth choose the successors to the Head of the Commonwealth since the office is not inherited. Since there is no term restriction after taking office, the incumbent is essentially appointed for life.

When Elizabeth II entered her 90s in 2018, there had long been debates over who should succeed him as the third Head of the Commonwealth, either Prince Charles or someone else. According to the London Declaration, both republics and kingdoms that are not Commonwealth countries are permitted to recognize the monarch as Head of the Commonwealth without also acknowledging him or her as the head of state of their respective governments. There have been conflicting statements on how successors to the position of Head of the Commonwealth are chosen, despite the fact that each Commonwealth realm's laws on royal titles and styles made Head of the Commonwealth part of the Queen's full title[citation needed] and Queen Elizabeth II declared in 1958 through the Letters Patent creating Prince Charles as Prince of Wales that Charles and his heirs and successors shall be future heads of the Commonwealth. While the Commonwealth Secretariat said that the heads of state and government of the Commonwealth would choose any successor jointly,

The Queen visited every Commonwealth nation between February 1952 and 2015, when she last traveled abroad, with the exception of Cameroon and Rwanda. She also made close to 200 journeys and visits to Commonwealth and UK Overseas Territories. These travels, many of which were made during Cold War competition and tensions over decolonization, tried to keep the Commonwealth together in spite of its ethnic and ideological conflicts.

Following the 2018 Commonwealth Heads of Government Meeting, Commonwealth leaders announced Prince Charles will take over as the organization's leader going forward, however the position would not pass through the family. As a result, Charles will automatically succeed the Queen as Head of the Commonwealth following her passing.

Queen's Message 2015

One simple lesson from history is that when people come together to talk, to exchange ideas and to develop common goals, wonderful things can happen. So many of the world's greatest technological and industrial achievements have begun as partnerships between families, countries, and even continents. But, as we are often reminded, the opposite can also be true. When common goals fall apart, so does the exchange of ideas. And if people no longer trust or understand each other, the talking will soon stop too.

In the Commonwealth we are a group of 53 nations of dramatically different sizes and climates. But over the years, drawing on our shared history, we have seen and acted upon the huge advantages of mutual co-operation and understanding, for the benefit of our countries and the people who live in them. Not only are there tremendous rewards for this co-operation, but through dialogue we protect ourselves against the dangers that can so easily arise from a failure to talk or to see the other person's point of view.

Indeed, it seems to me that now, in the second decade of the 21st century, what we share through being members of the Commonwealth is more important and worthier of protection than perhaps at any other time in the Commonwealth's existence. We are guardians of a precious flame, and it is our duty not only to keep it burning brightly but to keep it replenished for the decades ahead.

With this in mind, I think it apt that on this day we celebrate 'A Young Commonwealth' and all that it has to offer. As a concept that is unique in human history, the Commonwealth can only flourish if its ideas and ideals continue to be young and fresh and relevant to all generations.

The youthfulness and vitality that motivate our collective endeavours were seen in abundance last year in Glasgow. They will be seen again in a few months' time when young leaders from islands and continents gather to make new friendships and to work on exciting initiatives that can help to build a safer world for future generations. And last November in India, talented young scientists from universities and research institutes conferred with eminent professors and pioneers of discovery at the Commonwealth Science Conference where together they shared thoughts on insights and inventions that promise a more sustainable future.

These are stirring examples of what is meant by 'A Young Commonwealth'. It is a globally diverse and inclusive community that opens up new possibilities for development through trust and encouragement. Commonwealth Day provides each of us, as members of this worldwide family, with a chance to recommit ourselves to upholding the values of the Commonwealth Charter.

It has the power to enrich us all, but, just as importantly in an uncertain world, it gives us a good reason to keep talking.

Queen's Message 2014

In July this year, the opening of the 20th Commonwealth Games will be marked by the arrival in Glasgow of the baton that started its journey from Buckingham Palace five months ago.

Many of us are following closely the news of the baton relay as it passes through the 70 countries and territories whose teams will gather for the Games. The images bring vividly to life what we mean by the Commonwealth family: it is wonderful to see the warmth, shared endeavour and goodwill as the baton is passed through the hands of many thousands of people.

Affinities of history and inheritance from the past are strong, yet we are bound together by a sense that the Commonwealth is a powerful influence of good for the future. People of all ages from different cultures are weaving an ever-growing network of links which connect us in our diversity and our common purpose. It is this unity that is expressed in this year's theme: 'Team Commonwealth'. While national teams will be concentrating on the competition in August, Team Commonwealth will have a longer focus, working together to achieve a more enduring success.

Experiences of life differ widely throughout the Commonwealth, and we each make contributions from sometimes very different viewpoints. But we are committed to the same goals. Together we offer each other encouragement and draw strength from this mutual support. The understanding that we belong together, and are able, through teamwork, to achieve far more than we could do alone, has always been at the heart of our approach. For all of us this is now captured in the Commonwealth Charter which sets out the values and principles which guide and motivate us.

This year, more children and young people are participating in Commonwealth Day celebrations. Advances in technology enable us to reach a greater number of young people in schools, on-line using the 'Commonwealth Class' initiative, and through events in local communities where the Commonwealth flag is being raised. I am delighted that in this, the year of 'Team Commonwealth', we will be working to build a brighter, united future in which every one of us can play a part and share in its rewards.

Chapter five

The commonwealth games

Athletes from the Commonwealth of Nations compete in the quadrennial international multisport Commonwealth Games. The Commonwealth Games Federation, with headquarters in London, England, is in charge of running the Commonwealth Games.

Astley Cooper, an Australian who advocated for the holding of sporting tournaments to show the unity of the British Empire, initially raised the notion of such games in 1891. A "Festival of the Empire" was held in 1911 to commemorate King George V's coronation. Teams from the UK, Australasia (Australia and New Zealand), Canada, South Africa, and South Africa took part in a number of competitions in the sports of swimming, boxing, wrestling, and athletics. The first British Empire Games were held in 1930 in Hamilton, Canada. 400 competitors from 11 nations competed in athletics, lawn bowls, boxing, swimming, and wrestling, and the English team won the most medals overall. Only the swimming events had women competitors. It was decided that the Games would take place in various Commonwealth towns every four years, ideally in the middle of the Olympic Games. The initial plans for the second British Empire Games in 1934 were for Johannesburg, South Africa. The Games were relocated to London because to worries about South Africa's apartheid legislation and associated worries about bias towards athletes of color. There were sixteen nations represented, and athletics included women for the first time. There was a 12-year break after the third Games, which were staged in Sydney in 1938, as a result of World War II. In 1950, the Games were revived in Auckland, New Zealand.

The first-time nations outside of the British Empire competed in the Olympics was during the Vancouver tournament in 1954. This history is reflected in the new name, "British Empire and Commonwealth Games." Twenty-four nations took part, and for the first time in the Games' history, live telecasts were available. The one-mile running competition was dubbed the "Miracle Mile" because gold medallist Roger Bannister of England and silver medalist John Landy of Australia both ran sub-four-minute miles, marking the first time two runners had done so in the same race. The Queen's Baton Relay, in which the Queen's Baton is passed from person to person in a relay beginning at Buckingham Palace in London and finishing at the Games site, made its debut in 1958 in Cardiff, Wales. The first time that badminton and shooting were included as sports was in the 1966 Games in Kingston, Jamaica.

The 1970 Games in Edinburgh, Scotland, included competition from 42 nations. The event was renamed the "British Commonwealth Games," and competitions were held for the first time using metric measurements rather than imperial measurements. Queen Elizabeth II attended these games for the first time as the leader of the Commonwealth. Nigeria boycotted the 1978 Games, the first to be referred to as "Commonwealth Games," which were held in Edmonton, Canada, in opposition to New Zealand's participation in sports with South Africa during the apartheid period. Political boycotts continued to plague the Olympics. Because the U.K. government refused to impose penalties on apartheid South Africa, 32 African, Asian, and Caribbean nations boycotted the 1986 Games in Edinburgh. As a result, only 26 countries participated. But the 1990 Auckland Games witnessed a comeback, with 55 nations taking part. After the end of apartheid, South Africa returned to the Commonwealth Games in Victoria, Canada, in 1994. Hong Kong took part in the Games for the last time before handing over sovereignty to China in 1997.

Team sports were introduced in the 1998 Games in Kuala Lumpur, Malaysia, the first Games to be held in Asia, where 70 nations fought for a share of the medals. Cricket was very recently included to the Games—in 1998—despite having a significant connection to the British Commonwealth. (Nevertheless, it was not a part of the 2002 or following Games; however, women's T20 cricket will be a part of the 2022 Games.) In order to concentrate on the Sahara Cup, a bilateral series contested between the two nations, India and Pakistan—the two nations with the largest cricket TV audience—sent depleted teams to the 1998 Olympics. The cricket medals were won by South Africa, Australia, and New Zealand, all of whom had strong squads. The 2010 Games were the first to take place in a Commonwealth nation and were hosted in Delhi, India. With an equal number of events (and medals) for men and women for the first time, the 2018 Games in Gold Coast, Australia, demonstrated how far the event has advanced in terms of gender inclusion. England's Birmingham was selected as the host city for the 2022 Olympics.

Prior to the main Commonwealth Games, a separate tournament known as the Commonwealth Paraplegic Games was held from 1962 until 1974. After 1974, they were abandoned, but in 1994, they were reinstated as demonstration sports in the main Games. The main Commonwealth Games have incorporated para sports completely since 2002, enabling para athletes to compete as members of the main national teams. With a total of 2,416 medals throughout all Games editions until 2018, including 932 golds, Australia is in first place, followed by England, Canada, and India. The only nations that have competed in every Games are Australia, Canada, England, New Zealand, Scotland, and Wales.

References

- Commonwealth network,

- The Future Role of the Commonwealth, Foreign Affairs Committee, First Report of

- 1995-96, HC 45, 27 March 1996, para 143.

- WorldData.info

- Commonwealth Secretariat Communications and Public Affairs Division Marlborough House Pall Mall, London

- Commonwealth Secretariat. Archived from the original on 31 March 2012. Retrieved 23 March 2009.

- Royal Insight. September 2006. p. 3. Archived from the original on 19 November 2000

- commonwealthofnations.org/commonwealth/commonwealth-membership/withdrawals-and-suspension/